PETER PAUPER PRESS
Fine Books and Gifts Since 1928

Our Company

In 1928, at the age of twenty-two, Peter Beilenson began printing books on a small press in the basement of his parents' home in Larchmont, New York. Peter—and later, his wife, Edna—sought to create fine books that sold at "prices even a pauper could afford."

Today, still family owned and operated, Peter Pauper Press continues to honor our founders' legacy—and our customers' expectations—of beauty, quality, and value.

———

Illustrations used under license from Shutterstock.com

Designed by Margaret Rubiano

Printed in China
7 6 5 4 3 2 1

Visit us at www.peterpauper.com

CONTENTS

INTRODUCTION

t's harder than ever to catch some zzzs in today's plugged-in world, with our many devices, 24/7 work emails, and binge-streaming, not to mention our personal cares and worries.

This little logbook can help. It's packed with information about sleep and ideas for getting better rest.

More important, it allows you to record your nightly routines for more than a month, in order to identify how your rest relates to certain days, meal times, foods, drinks, medications, activities, and so on.

You'll also find space to record your dreams. They may reveal deeper insights into your well-being.

Keep this sleep tracker on your nightstand and bring it with you when you meet with your health care providers.

We hope it helps you sleep like a log!

I CANNOT
SLEEP A WINK.

ALEXANDER POPE

HOW MUCH SLEEP DO WE NEED?

Here are minimal guidelines recommended by the National Heart, Lung, and Blood Institute (NHLB), part of the U.S. Department of Health and Human Services and National Institutes of Health:

AGE	RECOMMENDED AMOUNT OF SLEEP
NEWBORNS	*16–18 hours a day*
PRESCHOOL-AGED CHILDREN	*11–12 hours a day*
SCHOOL-AGED CHILDREN	*At least 10 hours a day*
TEENS	*9–10 hours a day*
ADULTS (INCLUDING THE ELDERLY)	*7–8 hours a day*

Note that these are minimal recommendations. The National Sleep Foundation offers slightly different guidelines. Other sources urge us to grab *more zzzs*. It's interesting to note that elite athletes require 10 to 12 hours of sleep per night (plus naps in some cases!) for top performance.

The NHLB advises keeping a sleep diary (such as this logbook; log pages start on page 19) if you are concerned about how much rest you're getting. Share the information with your health care provider.

If you think you're getting the right amount of sleep, but still feel tired, tell your doctor. It may indicate a sleep disorder.

I'M IN LOVE WITH MY BED, BUT MY ALARM CLOCK WON'T ALLOW US TO BE TOGETHER.

MY SLEEP PROFILE

What keeps you up at night?

- [ ] I am a night owl and like to stay up late.
- [ ] I like to watch TV in bed.
- [ ] I must have my phone with me at all times.
- [ ] I like late-night snacks.
- [ ] I like late-night drinks.
- [ ] I like late-night nicotine.
- [ ] I'm caffeinated.
- [ ] Pizza guy delivering a late-night order to the wrong house—mine.
- [ ] I get charley horses.
- [ ] My spouse snores.
- [ ] My spouse uses a sleep apnea device . . . I'm sleeping with Darth Vader.
- [ ] Recycling poachers rifle through our bin of cans and bottles in the middle of the night and wake me up.
- [ ] I'm worried that my new neighbor is a vampire.
- [ ] I just like to worry.
- [ ] I have to pee a lot.
- [ ] I heard a weird noise in the walls . . . I think.
- [ ] My cat attacks my toes.
- [ ] My dog passes gas.
- [ ] My spouse takes all the covers.
- [ ] I have hot flashes and arctic chills.

☐ The lights are always on in that place down the street—I wonder if it's a meth lab.

☐ The neighbor's car alarm goes off.

☐ The morning paper delivery guy has his radio cranked up a thousand decibels.

☐ I am an early bird and like to get a jump on the day. At 4 A.M.

MY BED IS A MAGICAL PLACE
WHERE I SUDDENLY REMEMBER
EVERYTHING THAT I WAS
SUPPOSED TO DO.

SLEEP FACTS: FROM A TO ZZZS

A. Sleep may make up the most important one-third of your day.

B. When we sleep, we alternate REM (Rapid Eye Movement) sleep with non-REM sleep. These two kinds of sleep alternate through the night.

C. Non-REM sleep consists of three distinct stages. See page 10 for more information.

D. Our brains remain active as we sleep, even as our bodies rest.

E. People should naturally feel their drowsiest between midnight and 7:00 A.M.

F. You may also feel drowsy between 1:00 P.M. and 4:00 P.M.

G. We are the least alert during early morning hours.

H. If you suffer from inflammation or infection, you may need extra sleep to recover, in which case your immune system may produce **cytokines**, hormones which may cause you to become sleepy.

I. Infants (when they actually sleep!) spend more time in REM (Rapid Eye Movement) sleep (see page 10) than anyone else—about half or more of their sleep time.

J. REM sleep—when dreaming takes place—decreases as we become older, to about one-fifth of our sleep time. REM sleep excites the areas of the brain we use in making memories and learning.

K. Deep stage 3 non-REM sleep prompts the production of essential growth hormones in children.

L. Stage 3 non-REM sleep is also recuperative and aids in the renewal of cells and tissues in children and adults.

M. Our bodies produce a nucleoside called **adenosine** which may affect sleep patterns. When we're awake, adenosine accumulates in our blood. When we sleep, adenosine is metabolized.

N. Ever wonder how your morning coffee wakes you up? Some experts believe caffeine blocks the sleep-inciting cell receptors of adenosine.

O. Your body also produces the hormone **melatonin**, which helps make us sleepy. Its production decreases as we get older, leading some researchers to believe it may be associated with aging. Another substance you may have heard about, **serotonin**, is one of the building blocks of melatonin.

P. Why in the world are we online well past our bedtime? *Sleep Smarter* author Shawn Stevenson tells us it relates to **dopamine**, the brain chemical "that's all about seeking." Searching the Internet is an inexhaustible lure for us; our brains are oh-so-easily hooked on finding the next cute cat, sloth, or hedgehog picture. Why not? Each one gives us a feel-good "hit."

Q. Ironically, the concept of Google and a searchable World Wide Web came to Larry Page, Google co-founder, in a dream.

R. The TVs and devices we love emit stimulating blue light, which suppresses melatonin, contributing to our inability to get quality shut-eye!

S. Sleep may affect your weight. When we sleep well, production of the hormone **grehlin**, an appetite stimulant, is *decreased*, while production of the appetite suppressor **leptin** *increases*. When we don't sleep, the opposite may occur and we eat more.

T. We *used* to get more rest. According to the National Institutes of Health, in 1910, most people slept nine hours a night. Now we sleep fewer than seven.

U. Lack of sleep may increase one's chances of developing depression, high blood pressure, diabetes, and other disorders.

V. Why do children—and adults—sleep easier with and after a warm bath? Because the bath causes one's body temperature to rise and, after you get out of the tub, decrease in a way that echoes the experience of falling asleep.

W. Insomnia may simply be caused by a deficiency in magnesium. Your doctor can determine if this is true for you.

X. Half of all adults snore.

Y. The disorder **sleep apnea** is as common as asthma.

Z. Z is for zombies . . . don't be one! Gift yourself some zzzs and get a good night's rest!

YOU CALL IT SLEEP.
I CALL IT KEEPING REALITY AT BAY.

THOSE MYSTERIOUS SLEEP STAGES EXPLAINED

NON-REM (RAPID EYE MOVEMENT) OR NREM SLEEP

STAGE 1. The first ten minutes or so: Light's out. It's bedtime. The sandman stops by. You start to feel sleepy. Sooo sleeepy. And then you are sleeping . . . lightly. Your muscles relax. And sometimes twitch.

STAGE 2. The next twenty minutes: Your eye movement stops. Your brain waves slooowww— and yet occasionally have a burst of activity!

STAGE 3. Now you're in the Land of Nod. You sleep . . . deeply. Ah. Restorative Stage 3 sleep. Repair of cells and tissues is underway. Now everything decelerates: your brain waves, heart rate, respiratory system. You're relaxxxed.

REM (RAPID EYE MOVEMENT) SLEEP

STAGE 4. About an hour and a half after Stage 1, you begin to dream. (Yes, the giant platypus is after you again!) Your eyes move rapidly behind your closed eyelids. (That's why it's called Rapid Eye Movement Sleep.) Bodily functions, such as breathing, heart rate, and blood pressure, are irregular. Limbs may be paralyzed for short periods of time.

But you and the platypus become friends . . . and you return to lighter Stage 1 Sleep, which lasts longer this time around, then you're on to Stage 2 and 3 again, then 4 and REM Sleep. Ah, and this time raccoons are rambling through your reveries.

Thus, REM Sleep alternates with non-REM Sleep throughout the night. We complete several cycles of these stages in one night's sleep, with each cycle taking up to about two hours.

Sleep experts recommend trying to plan your sleep around these sleep cycles. For example, if you can get to bed by 11:00 P.M. and wake at 7:00 A.M. without interruptions during the night, you might get in four good cycles of sleep. Try counting back eight hours from when you have to get up and make that your bedtime.

BE QUIET, LIFE.
I'M TRYING TO SLEEP.

SLEEP DISORDERS AND THEIR SYMPTOMS

Here is some basic information about several types of sleep disorders. If you or a loved one is experiencing any of these symptoms, consult your physician.

- **INSOMNIA.** When you are unable to get sufficient rest on a regular basis, because you have trouble falling asleep or have trouble getting back to sleep after waking during the night. Experts suggest leaving your bedroom and participating in a calming activity. Try journaling, sketching, coloring, needlepoint, knitting, or reading a print book or magazine. Go back to bed when you're sleepy.

- **SLEEP APNEA.** Also known as sleep-disordered breathing. You're breathing but you're not getting enough air into your lungs and oxygen into your blood, due to recurring upper-airway blockages. Your brain prompts you to wake up so you can start breathing again, and you do, with sudden coughs or snorting. This happens over and over again through the night. This can be serious. Such sleep disruption and deprivation affects all you do, and increases the chances for accidents. A Continuous Positive Airway Pressure (CPAP) machine may be needed to help you breathe. Note: Snoring is associated with sleep apnea, but not all snorers have this disorder.

- **NARCOLEPSY.** You can barely stay awake during the day. You experience "sleep attacks" and fall asleep at inappropriate times. When you do, you may fall right into REM dream sleep. Health care providers may suggest daytime naps to help curb this disorder. Narcolepsy may be accompanied by **cataplexy**, sudden muscle paralysis that lasts a minute or two. You remain cognizant of what is happening, but you are immobile. You may fall asleep after such an episode. Narcolepsy may also be accompanied by **sleep paralysis**: as you go to sleep or wake up, you are incapable of movement or speech. You may experience powerful dreams that closely resemble real life. Narcolepsy is more common in some cultures, for example, Japan and the U.S., than others.

- **PARASOMNIAS.** These are atypical sleep behaviors, such as talking in one's sleep, sleepwalking, and night terrors. Safety is a major concern here for children or adults who behave in this way, or for family members of those affected. Parasomnias are more common in children than adults.

- **RESTLESS LEG SYNDROME (RLS).** A tingling in your legs or calves. May affect arms. May be relieved by rubbing or moving affected limbs. Affects about 10 percent of the population. Certain deficiencies or medications may trigger RLS. It may also be an inherited condition. Avoid caffeine.

LAUGH AND THE WORLD
LAUGHS WITH YOU. SNORE
AND YOU SNORE ALONE.

ANTHONY BURGESS

Make your bedroom a refuge from the world.

- **Keep it comfy.** Experts say the ideal sleeping temperature ranges from about 60 to 66 degrees, as much as possible. Cold? Try wearing socks.

- **Décor.** Use restful, calming colors such as soft gray-blues and greens.

- **Furnishings:** Select pieces you love. Hang artwork that makes you happy.

- **Darkness.** Artificial light hinders the production of melatonin, the hormone that helps trigger sleepiness. Block as much artificial light as possible. For example, do you still use a digital alarm clock? Turn it to the wall. Try turning off the nightlight or use dim red lights, which are less disturbing to our systems. Street lamps from outside shining in? Try blackout window treatments.

- **Select the most comfortable sleepwear you can.** Think natural, breathable fabrics that are free of synthetics.

- **Improve air quality.** Bring in plants, such as English ivy, to help purify your bedroom environment.

- **Try to go to bed and get up at consistent times.** Get a shot of sunlight early in the day to help re-set your biological clock.

SORRY, I CAN'T.
MY BED NEEDS ME.

FOOD, DRINK, AND NICOTINE

Watch your intake, especially before bedtime.

- **Caffeine.** Do not consume caffeinated beverages (coffee, tea, cola) or food (chocolate!) less than four hours before you go to bed. Note: The effects of caffeine may even take as long as six to eight hours to wear off completely.

- **Food.** No large meals right before bed. Finish at least 90 minutes before you retire. No spicy stuff.

- **Booze.** No. Unless you feel the need to wake up at 3:00 A.M. Alcohol inhibits deep sleep and REM sleep. If you must imbibe, do it several hours before bed (happy hour!), then hydrate with water.

- **Smoking.** Put it out at least an hour before you hit the hay. Heavy smokers may wake up earlier simply because their bodies are going through nicotine withdrawal.

- **Medications.** If you believe your medications may be keeping you from sleeping (and many do), talk to your health care provider.

DEAR SLEEP, I KNOW WE HAD
OUR ISSUES WHEN I WAS YOUNG,
BUT I LOVE YOU NOW.

SLEEP AND EXERCISE

Exercise is good for wakefulness and for sleep.

- Move! Just do it! Whether it's walking, climbing the stairs, yoga, gardening, or housework, move throughout your day. You'll sleep better.

- And, in turn, a good night's sleep means repair, renewal, and toning of your muscles. You'll gain more energy for the next day.

- If possible, it's better not to exercise vigorously shortly before bed. However, experts say those who work out any time of the day do sleep better than those who don't exercise at all.

IF WE WERE MEANT
TO POP OUT OF BED,
WE'D SLEEP IN TOASTERS.

BID BLUE ADIEU

Unplug to power down.

- TVs, phones, tablets, e-readers, pads, pods, games. Our electronic devices emit stimulating blue light. During the day, blue wavelengths keep us alert and boost our mood. But blue light also prohibits secretion of melatonin and tricks our bodies into staying awake. Turn off devices at least 30 to 90 minutes before bed to give your body a chance to recover.

- What? You say you must have your phone by your side? Think about it: Why are you giving others control over your quality of life?

- Try to keep the electronics out of the bedroom. They (along with other appliances, such as AC units) emit EMFs (electric and magnetic fields), the effects of which are controversial. According to the U.S. National Institute of Environmental Health Sciences (NIEHS), in general, association of EMFs with health problems is insubstantial. However, research is ongoing and the Institute recommends "continued education on practical ways of reducing exposures to EMFs."

SLEEP IS THE
BEST MEDITATION.
THE DALAI LAMA

DREAM ON

Why do we dream? Theories about the purposes and benefits of dreams are plentiful. Dreams may serve many functions, from nurturing our brains to helping us work through emotions. They may help us organize memories. They may help us envisage creative solutions to problems.

Dreams may be quite puzzling. Dream dictionaries can help us interpret them. For example, according to *Llewellyn's Complete Dictionary of Dreams*, if you dream of a doorbell, it may indicate you're "being alerted that something new is on its way into your experience."

LAST NIGHT I DREAMED
I ATE A 10-POUND MARSHMALLOW,
AND WHEN I WOKE UP THE
PILLOW WAS GONE.

TOMMY COOPER

SLEEP LOG
PAGES

Use the following pages to record your rest, your dreams, and daily and bedtime activities that may affect your sleep.

CARPE NOCTEM!
SEIZE THE NIGHT.

DATE _____ DAY OF THE WEEK _____

☀ MORNING

When I went to bed last night .... When I woke up this morning ....

About how long I think it took me to fall asleep last night ....

Sleep disruptions ....

....

....

How long it took me to go back to sleep ....

Total hours I slept last night (approximate) ....

How I feel this morning

☐ Great ☐ Good ☐ Tired but functioning

☐ Very tired ☐ Not well

Notes ....

....

....

☾ DREAMS

Describe or draw your dreams here

....

....

....

....

....

....

....

....

DAYTIME

How many caffeinated beverages, or foods containing caffeine, did you consume today? ....

At what time? ....

Medications or supplements taken today ....

....At what time? ....

Did you exercise today? ....When, what, and for how long? ....

....

Did you take any naps? ....When, and for how long? ....

Did you eat heavy meals or spicy foods? What kinds of foods? ....

Any alcoholic beverages consumed today? .... At what time? ....

Describe your day. Was it stimulating or stressful? ....

....

How was your mood? ....

Notes ....

BEDTIME

What did you eat or drink within the last three hours? ....

What medications are you taking before bedtime? ....

Before getting ready for bed, I

☐ Took a hot bath   ☐ Read a physical printed book

☐ Meditated   ☐ Other ....

☐ Used my cell phone or other electronic device

....

....

Notes ....

....

....

DATE _____ DAY OF THE WEEK _____

☀ MORNING

When I went to bed last night .... When I woke up this morning ....

About how long I think it took me to fall asleep last night ....

Sleep disruptions ....

....

....

How long it took me to go back to sleep ....

Total hours I slept last night (approximate) ....

How I feel this morning

☐ Great   ☐ Good   ☐ Tired but functioning

☐ Very tired   ☐ Not well

Notes ....

....

....

🌙 DREAMS

Describe or draw your dreams here

....

....

....

....

....

....

....

....

DAYTIME

How many caffeinated beverages, or foods containing caffeine, did you consume today? ....

At what time? ....

Medications or supplements taken today ....

....At what time? ....

Did you exercise today? ....When, what, and for how long? ....

....

Did you take any naps? ....When, and for how long? ....

Did you eat heavy meals or spicy foods? What kinds of foods? ....

Any alcoholic beverages consumed today? ....At what time? ....

Describe your day. Was it stimulating or stressful? ....

....

How was your mood? ....

Notes ....

BEDTIME

What did you eat or drink within the last three hours? ....

What medications are you taking before bedtime? ....

Before getting ready for bed, I

☐ Took a hot bath

☐ Meditated

☐ Used my cell phone or other electronic device

☐ Read a physical printed book

☐ Other ....

....

....

Notes ....

....

....

DATE _____ DAY OF THE WEEK _____

☀ MORNING

When I went to bed last night .... When I woke up this morning ....

About how long I think it took me to fall asleep last night ....

Sleep disruptions ....

....

....

How long it took me to go back to sleep ....

Total hours I slept last night (approximate) ....

How I feel this morning

☐ Great ☐ Good ☐ Tired but functioning

☐ Very tired ☐ Not well

Notes ....

....

....

🌙 DREAMS

Describe or draw your dreams here

....

....

....

....

....

....

....

....

# DAYTIME

How many caffeinated beverages, or foods containing caffeine, did you consume today? ....

At what time? ....

Medications or supplements taken today ....

....At what time? ....

Did you exercise today? ....When, what, and for how long? ....

....

Did you take any naps? ....When, and for how long? ....

Did you eat heavy meals or spicy foods? What kinds of foods? ....

Any alcoholic beverages consumed today? ....At what time? ....

Describe your day. Was it stimulating or stressful? ....

....

How was your mood? ....

Notes ....

BEDTIME

What did you eat or drink within the last three hours? ....

What medications are you taking before bedtime? ....

Before getting ready for bed, I

☐ Took a hot bath

☐ Meditated

☐ Used my cell phone or other electronic device

☐ Read a physical printed book

☐ Other ....

....

....

Notes ....

....

....

DATE _____ DAY OF THE WEEK _____

☀ MORNING

When I went to bed last night ....When I woke up this morning ....

About how long I think it took me to fall asleep last night ....

Sleep disruptions ....

....

....

How long it took me to go back to sleep ....

Total hours I slept last night (approximate) ....

How I feel this morning

☐ Great ☐ Good ☐ Tired but functioning

☐ Very tired ☐ Not well

Notes ....

....

....

🌙 DREAMS

Describe or draw your dreams here

DAYTIME

How many caffeinated beverages, or foods containing caffeine, did you consume today? ....

At what time? ....

Medications or supplements taken today ....

....At what time? ....

Did you exercise today? ....When, what, and for how long? ....

....

Did you take any naps? ....When, and for how long? ....

Did you eat heavy meals or spicy foods? What kinds of foods? ....

Any alcoholic beverages consumed today? ....At what time? ....

Describe your day. Was it stimulating or stressful? ....

....

How was your mood? ....

Notes ....

BEDTIME

What did you eat or drink within the last three hours? ....

What medications are you taking before bedtime? ....

Before getting ready for bed, I

☐ Took a hot bath   ☐ Read a physical printed book

☐ Meditated   ☐ Other ....

☐ Used my cell phone or other electronic device

....

Notes ....

....

....

DATE _____ DAY OF THE WEEK _____

☀ MORNING

When I went to bed last night .... When I woke up this morning ....

About how long I think it took me to fall asleep last night ....

Sleep disruptions ....

....

....

How long it took me to go back to sleep ....

Total hours I slept last night (approximate) ....

How I feel this morning

☐ Great ☐ Good ☐ Tired but functioning

☐ Very tired ☐ Not well

Notes ....

....

....

☾ DREAMS

Describe or draw your dreams here

....

....

....

....

....

....

....

....

# DAYTIME

How many caffeinated beverages, or foods containing caffeine, did you consume today? ....

At what time? ....

Medications or supplements taken today ....

....At what time? ....

Did you exercise today? ....When, what, and for how long? ....

....

Did you take any naps? ....When, and for how long? ....

Did you eat heavy meals or spicy foods? What kinds of foods? ....

Any alcoholic beverages consumed today? ....At what time? ....

Describe your day. Was it stimulating or stressful? ....

....

How was your mood? ....

Notes ....

BEDTIME

What did you eat or drink within the last three hours? ....

What medications are you taking before bedtime? ....

Before getting ready for bed, I

☐ Took a hot bath

☐ Meditated

☐ Used my cell phone or other electronic device

☐ Read a physical printed book

☐ Other ....

....

Notes ....

....

....

....

DATE _____ DAY OF THE WEEK _____

☀ MORNING

When I went to bed last night .... When I woke up this morning ....

About how long I think it took me to fall asleep last night ....

Sleep disruptions ....

....

....

How long it took me to go back to sleep ....

Total hours I slept last night (approximate) ....

How I feel this morning

☐ Great ☐ Good ☐ Tired but functioning

☐ Very tired ☐ Not well

Notes ....

....

....

☾ DREAMS

Describe or draw your dreams here

....

....

....

....

....

....

....

....

 # DAYTIME

How many caffeinated beverages, or foods containing caffeine, did you consume today? ....

At what time? ....

Medications or supplements taken today ....

.... At what time? ....

Did you exercise today? .... When, what, and for how long? ....

....

Did you take any naps? .... When, and for how long? ....

Did you eat heavy meals or spicy foods? What kinds of foods? ....

Any alcoholic beverages consumed today? .... At what time? ....

Describe your day. Was it stimulating or stressful? ....

....

How was your mood? ....

Notes ....

BEDTIME

What did you eat or drink within the last three hours? ....

What medications are you taking before bedtime? ....

Before getting ready for bed, I

☐ Took a hot bath ☐ Read a physical printed book

☐ Meditated ☐ Other ....

☐ Used my cell phone or other electronic device

....

Notes ....

....

....

DATE _____ DAY OF THE WEEK _____

☀ MORNING

When I went to bed last night .... When I woke up this morning ....

About how long I think it took me to fall asleep last night ....

Sleep disruptions ....

....

....

How long it took me to go back to sleep ....

Total hours I slept last night (approximate) ....

How I feel this morning

☐ Great ☐ Good ☐ Tired but functioning

☐ Very tired ☐ Not well

Notes ....

....

....

☾ DREAMS

Describe or draw your dreams here

....

....

....

....

....

....

....

....

....

# DAYTIME

How many caffeinated beverages, or foods containing caffeine, did you consume today? ....

At what time? ....

Medications or supplements taken today ....

.... At what time? ....

Did you exercise today? .... When, what, and for how long? ....

....

Did you take any naps? .... When, and for how long? ....

Did you eat heavy meals or spicy foods? What kinds of foods? ....

Any alcoholic beverages consumed today? .... At what time? ....

Describe your day. Was it stimulating or stressful? ....

....

How was your mood? ....

Notes ....

BEDTIME

What did you eat or drink within the last three hours? ....

What medications are you taking before bedtime? ....

Before getting ready for bed, I

☐ Took a hot bath   ☐ Read a physical printed book

☐ Meditated   ☐ Other ....

☐ Used my cell phone or other electronic device

....

....

Notes ....

....

....

☀ MORNING

When I went to bed last night .... When I woke up this morning ....

About how long I think it took me to fall asleep last night ....

Sleep disruptions ....

....

....

How long it took me to go back to sleep ....

Total hours I slept last night (approximate) ....

How I feel this morning

☐ Great ☐ Good ☐ Tired but functioning

☐ Very tired ☐ Not well

Notes ....

....

....

🌙 DREAMS

Describe or draw your dreams here

....

....

....

....

....

....

....

....

# DAYTIME

How many caffeinated beverages, or foods containing caffeine, did you consume today? ....

At what time? ....

Medications or supplements taken today ....

.... At what time? ....

Did you exercise today? .... When, what, and for how long? ....

....

Did you take any naps? .... When, and for how long? ....

Did you eat heavy meals or spicy foods? What kinds of foods? ....

Any alcoholic beverages consumed today? .... At what time? ....

Describe your day. Was it stimulating or stressful? ....

....

How was your mood? ....

Notes ....

BEDTIME

What did you eat or drink within the last three hours? ....

What medications are you taking before bedtime? ....

Before getting ready for bed, I

☐ Took a hot bath   ☐ Read a physical printed book

☐ Meditated   ☐ Other ....

☐ Used my cell phone or other electronic device

....

Notes ....

....

....

DATE _____ DAY OF THE WEEK _____

☀ MORNING

When I went to bed last night .... When I woke up this morning ....

About how long I think it took me to fall asleep last night ....

Sleep disruptions ....

....

....

How long it took me to go back to sleep ....

Total hours I slept last night (approximate) ....

How I feel this morning

☐ Great ☐ Good ☐ Tired but functioning

☐ Very tired ☐ Not well

Notes ....

....

....

🌙 DREAMS

Describe or draw your dreams here

....

....

....

....

....

....

....

....

....

....

 DAYTIME

How many caffeinated beverages, or foods containing caffeine, did you consume today? ....

At what time? ....

Medications or supplements taken today ....

....At what time? ....

Did you exercise today? ....When, what, and for how long? ....

....

Did you take any naps? ....When, and for how long? ....

Did you eat heavy meals or spicy foods? What kinds of foods? ....

Any alcoholic beverages consumed today? ....At what time? ....

Describe your day. Was it stimulating or stressful? ....

....

How was your mood? ....

Notes ....

BEDTIME

What did you eat or drink within the last three hours? ....

What medications are you taking before bedtime? ....

Before getting ready for bed, I

☐ Took a hot bath   ☐ Read a physical printed book

☐ Meditated   ☐ Other ....

☐ Used my cell phone or other electronic device

....

....

Notes ....

....

....

....

DATE _____ DAY OF THE WEEK _____

☀ MORNING

When I went to bed last night .... When I woke up this morning ....

About how long I think it took me to fall asleep last night ....

Sleep disruptions ....

....

....

How long it took me to go back to sleep ....

Total hours I slept last night (approximate) ....

How I feel this morning

☐ Great   ☐ Good   ☐ Tired but functioning

☐ Very tired   ☐ Not well

Notes ....

....

🌙 DREAMS

Describe or draw your dreams here

....

....

....

....

....

....

....

....

....

# DAYTIME

How many caffeinated beverages, or foods containing caffeine, did you consume today? ....

At what time? ....

Medications or supplements taken today ....

....At what time? ....

Did you exercise today? ....When, what, and for how long? ....

....

Did you take any naps? ....When, and for how long? ....

Did you eat heavy meals or spicy foods? What kinds of foods? ....

Any alcoholic beverages consumed today? ....At what time? ....

Describe your day. Was it stimulating or stressful? ....

....

How was your mood? ....

Notes ....

BEDTIME

What did you eat or drink within the last three hours? ....

What medications are you taking before bedtime? ....

Before getting ready for bed, I

☐ Took a hot bath

☐ Meditated

☐ Used my cell phone or other electronic device

☐ Read a physical printed book

☐ Other ....

....

Notes ....

....

....

....

DATE _____ DAY OF THE WEEK _____

☀ MORNING

When I went to bed last night .... When I woke up this morning ....

About how long I think it took me to fall asleep last night ....

Sleep disruptions ....

....

....

How long it took me to go back to sleep ....

Total hours I slept last night (approximate) ....

How I feel this morning

☐ Great   ☐ Good   ☐ Tired but functioning

☐ Very tired   ☐ Not well

Notes ....

....

....

🌙 DREAMS
Describe or draw your dreams here

....

....

....

....

....

....

....

....

....

....

# DAYTIME

How many caffeinated beverages, or foods containing caffeine, did you consume today? ....

At what time? ....

Medications or supplements taken today ....

.... At what time? ....

Did you exercise today? .... When, what, and for how long? ....

....

Did you take any naps? .... When, and for how long? ....

Did you eat heavy meals or spicy foods? What kinds of foods? ....

Any alcoholic beverages consumed today? .... At what time? ....

Describe your day. Was it stimulating or stressful? ....

....

How was your mood? ....

Notes ....

BEDTIME

What did you eat or drink within the last three hours? ....

What medications are you taking before bedtime? ....

Before getting ready for bed, I

☐ Took a hot bath

☐ Meditated

☐ Used my cell phone or other electronic device

☐ Read a physical printed book

☐ Other ....

....

Notes ....

....

....

....

DATE _____ DAY OF THE WEEK _____

☀ MORNING

When I went to bed last night .... When I woke up this morning ....

About how long I think it took me to fall asleep last night ....

Sleep disruptions ....

....

....

How long it took me to go back to sleep ....

Total hours I slept last night (approximate) ....

How I feel this morning

- ☐ Great ☐ Good ☐ Tired but functioning
- ☐ Very tired ☐ Not well

Notes ....

....

....

🌙 DREAMS

Describe or draw your dreams here

....

....

....

....

....

....

....

....

....

....

DAYTIME

How many caffeinated beverages, or foods containing caffeine, did you consume today? ....

At what time? ....

Medications or supplements taken today ....

....At what time? ....

Did you exercise today? ....When, what, and for how long? ....

....

Did you take any naps? ....When, and for how long? ....

Did you eat heavy meals or spicy foods? What kinds of foods? ....

Any alcoholic beverages consumed today? ....At what time? ....

Describe your day. Was it stimulating or stressful? ....

....

How was your mood? ....

Notes ....

BEDTIME

What did you eat or drink within the last three hours? ....

What medications are you taking before bedtime? ....

Before getting ready for bed, I

☐ Took a hot bath

☐ Meditated

☐ Used my cell phone or other electronic device

☐ Read a physical printed book

☐ Other ....

....

....

Notes ....

....

....

....

DATE _____ DAY OF THE WEEK _____

☀ MORNING

When I went to bed last night .... When I woke up this morning ....

About how long I think it took me to fall asleep last night ....

Sleep disruptions ....

....

....

How long it took me to go back to sleep ....

Total hours I slept last night (approximate) ....

How I feel this morning

☐ Great ☐ Good ☐ Tired but functioning

☐ Very tired ☐ Not well

Notes ....

....

....

🌙 DREAMS

Describe or draw your dreams here

....

....

....

....

....

....

....

....

....

....

# DAYTIME

How many caffeinated beverages, or foods containing caffeine, did you consume today? ....

At what time? ....

Medications or supplements taken today ....

.... At what time? ....

Did you exercise today? .... When, what, and for how long? ....

....

Did you take any naps? .... When, and for how long? ....

Did you eat heavy meals or spicy foods? What kinds of foods? ....

Any alcoholic beverages consumed today? .... At what time? ....

Describe your day. Was it stimulating or stressful? ....

....

How was your mood? ....

Notes ....

BEDTIME

What did you eat or drink within the last three hours? ....

What medications are you taking before bedtime? ....

Before getting ready for bed, I

☐ Took a hot bath   ☐ Read a physical printed book

☐ Meditated   ☐ Other ....

☐ Used my cell phone or other electronic device

....

....

Notes ....

....

....

....

DATE _____ DAY OF THE WEEK _____

☀ MORNING

When I went to bed last night .... When I woke up this morning ....

About how long I think it took me to fall asleep last night ....

Sleep disruptions ....

....

....

How long it took me to go back to sleep ....

Total hours I slept last night (approximate) ....

How I feel this morning

☐ Great ☐ Good ☐ Tired but functioning

☐ Very tired ☐ Not well

Notes ....

....

....

☾ DREAMS

Describe or draw your dreams here

....

....

....

....

....

....

....

....

 # DAYTIME

How many caffeinated beverages, or foods containing caffeine, did you consume today? ....

At what time? ....

Medications or supplements taken today ....

.... At what time? ....

Did you exercise today? .... When, what, and for how long? ....

....

Did you take any naps? .... When, and for how long? ....

Did you eat heavy meals or spicy foods? What kinds of foods? ....

Any alcoholic beverages consumed today? .... At what time? ....

Describe your day. Was it stimulating or stressful? ....

....

How was your mood? ....

Notes ....

BEDTIME

What did you eat or drink within the last three hours? ....

What medications are you taking before bedtime? ....

Before getting ready for bed, I

☐ Took a hot bath   ☐ Read a physical printed book

☐ Meditated   ☐ Other ....

☐ Used my cell phone or other electronic device

....

Notes ....

....

....

....

DATE _____ DAY OF THE WEEK _____

☀ MORNING

When I went to bed last night .... When I woke up this morning ....

About how long I think it took me to fall asleep last night ....

Sleep disruptions ....

....

....

How long it took me to go back to sleep ....

Total hours I slept last night (approximate) ....

How I feel this morning

☐ Great ☐ Good ☐ Tired but functioning

☐ Very tired ☐ Not well

Notes ....

....

....

☾ DREAMS

Describe or draw your dreams here

....

....

....

....

....

....

....

....

....

 # DAYTIME

How many caffeinated beverages, or foods containing caffeine, did you consume today? ....

At what time? ....

Medications or supplements taken today ....

....At what time? ....

Did you exercise today? .... When, what, and for how long? ....

....

Did you take any naps? .... When, and for how long? ....

Did you eat heavy meals or spicy foods? What kinds of foods? ....

Any alcoholic beverages consumed today? .... At what time? ....

Describe your day. Was it stimulating or stressful? ....

....

How was your mood? ....

Notes ....

BEDTIME

What did you eat or drink within the last three hours? ....

What medications are you taking before bedtime? ....

Before getting ready for bed, I

☐ Took a hot bath

☐ Meditated

☐ Used my cell phone or other electronic device

☐ Read a physical printed book

☐ Other ....

....

Notes ....

....

....

....

DATE _____ DAY OF THE WEEK _____

☀ MORNING

When I went to bed last night .... When I woke up this morning ....

About how long I think it took me to fall asleep last night ....

Sleep disruptions ....

....

....

How long it took me to go back to sleep ....

Total hours I slept last night (approximate) ....

How I feel this morning

☐ Great ☐ Good ☐ Tired but functioning

☐ Very tired ☐ Not well

Notes ....

....

....

☾ DREAMS

Describe or draw your dreams here

....

....

....

....

....

....

....

....

....

DAYTIME

How many caffeinated beverages, or foods containing caffeine, did you consume today? ....

At what time? ....

Medications or supplements taken today ....

.... At what time? ....

Did you exercise today? .... When, what, and for how long? ....

....

Did you take any naps? .... When, and for how long? ....

Did you eat heavy meals or spicy foods? What kinds of foods? ....

Any alcoholic beverages consumed today? .... At what time? ....

Describe your day. Was it stimulating or stressful? ....

....

How was your mood? ....

Notes ....

BEDTIME

What did you eat or drink within the last three hours? ....

What medications are you taking before bedtime? ....

Before getting ready for bed, I

☐ Took a hot bath ☐ Read a physical printed book

☐ Meditated ☐ Other ....

☐ Used my cell phone or other electronic device

....

....

Notes ....

....

....

....

DATE _____ DAY OF THE WEEK _____

☀ MORNING

When I went to bed last night .... When I woke up this morning ....

About how long I think it took me to fall asleep last night ....

Sleep disruptions ....

....

....

How long it took me to go back to sleep ....

Total hours I slept last night (approximate) ....

How I feel this morning

☐ Great   ☐ Good   ☐ Tired but functioning

☐ Very tired   ☐ Not well

Notes ....

....

....

☾ DREAMS

Describe or draw your dreams here

....

....

....

....

....

....

....

....

....

 DAYTIME

How many caffeinated beverages, or foods containing caffeine, did you consume today? ....

At what time? ....

Medications or supplements taken today ....

....At what time? ....

Did you exercise today? ....When, what, and for how long? ....

....

Did you take any naps? ....When, and for how long? ....

Did you eat heavy meals or spicy foods? What kinds of foods? ....

Any alcoholic beverages consumed today? ....At what time? ....

Describe your day. Was it stimulating or stressful? ....

....

How was your mood? ....

Notes ....

BEDTIME

What did you eat or drink within the last three hours? ....

What medications are you taking before bedtime? ....

Before getting ready for bed, I

☐ Took a hot bath   ☐ Read a physical printed book

☐ Meditated   ☐ Other ....

☐ Used my cell phone or other electronic device

....

....

Notes ....

....

....

DATE _____ DAY OF THE WEEK _____

☀ MORNING

When I went to bed last night .... When I woke up this morning ....

About how long I think it took me to fall asleep last night ....

Sleep disruptions ....

....

....

How long it took me to go back to sleep ....

Total hours I slept last night (approximate) ....

How I feel this morning

☐ Great   ☐ Good   ☐ Tired but functioning

☐ Very tired   ☐ Not well

Notes ....

....

....

☾ DREAMS

Describe or draw your dreams here

....

....

....

....

....

....

....

....

 # DAYTIME

How many caffeinated beverages, or foods containing caffeine, did you consume today? ....

At what time? ....

Medications or supplements taken today ....

....At what time? ....

Did you exercise today? ....When, what, and for how long? ....

....

Did you take any naps? ....When, and for how long? ....

Did you eat heavy meals or spicy foods? What kinds of foods? ....

Any alcoholic beverages consumed today? .... At what time? ....

Describe your day. Was it stimulating or stressful? ....

....

How was your mood? ....

Notes ....

BEDTIME

What did you eat or drink within the last three hours? ....

What medications are you taking before bedtime? ....
Before getting ready for bed, I

☐ Took a hot bath   ☐ Read a physical printed book

☐ Meditated   ☐ Other ....

☐ Used my cell phone or other electronic device

....

Notes ....

....

....

....

DATE _____ DAY OF THE WEEK _____

☀ MORNING

When I went to bed last night .... When I woke up this morning ....

About how long I think it took me to fall asleep last night ....

Sleep disruptions ....

....

....

How long it took me to go back to sleep ....

Total hours I slept last night (approximate) ....

How I feel this morning

☐ Great ☐ Good ☐ Tired but functioning

☐ Very tired ☐ Not well

Notes ....

....

☾ DREAMS

Describe or draw your dreams here

....

....

....

....

....

....

....

....

DAYTIME

How many caffeinated beverages, or foods containing caffeine, did you consume today? ....

At what time? ....

Medications or supplements taken today ....

.... At what time? ....

Did you exercise today? .... When, what, and for how long? ....

....

Did you take any naps? .... When, and for how long? ....

Did you eat heavy meals or spicy foods? What kinds of foods? ....

Any alcoholic beverages consumed today? .... At what time? ....

Describe your day. Was it stimulating or stressful? ....

....

How was your mood? ....

Notes ....

BEDTIME

What did you eat or drink within the last three hours? ....

What medications are you taking before bedtime? ....
Before getting ready for bed, I

☐ Took a hot bath

☐ Meditated

☐ Used my cell phone or other electronic device

☐ Read a physical printed book

☐ Other ....

....

....

Notes ....

....

....

....

DATE _____ DAY OF THE WEEK _____

☀ MORNING

When I went to bed last night .... When I woke up this morning ....

About how long I think it took me to fall asleep last night ....

Sleep disruptions ....

....

....

How long it took me to go back to sleep ....

Total hours I slept last night (approximate) ....

How I feel this morning

◻ Great   ◻ Good   ◻ Tired but functioning

◻ Very tired   ◻ Not well

Notes ....

....

....

☾ DREAMS

Describe or draw your dreams here

....

....

....

....

....

....

....

....

....

# DAYTIME

How many caffeinated beverages, or foods containing caffeine, did you consume today? ....

At what time? ....

Medications or supplements taken today ....

.... At what time? ....

Did you exercise today? .... When, what, and for how long? ....

....

Did you take any naps? .... When, and for how long? ....

Did you eat heavy meals or spicy foods? What kinds of foods? ....

Any alcoholic beverages consumed today? .... At what time? ....

Describe your day. Was it stimulating or stressful? ....

....

How was your mood? ....

Notes ....

BEDTIME

What did you eat or drink within the last three hours? ....

What medications are you taking before bedtime? ....

Before getting ready for bed, I

☐ Took a hot bath   ☐ Read a physical printed book

☐ Meditated   ☐ Other ....

☐ Used my cell phone or other electronic device

....

Notes ....

....

....

DATE _____ DAY OF THE WEEK _____

☀ MORNING

When I went to bed last night .... When I woke up this morning ....

About how long I think it took me to fall asleep last night ....

Sleep disruptions ....

....

....

How long it took me to go back to sleep ....

Total hours I slept last night (approximate) ....

How I feel this morning

☐ Great ☐ Good ☐ Tired but functioning

☐ Very tired ☐ Not well

Notes ....

....

....

☾ DREAMS

Describe or draw your dreams here

....

....

....

....

....

....

....

....

....

 **DAYTIME**

How many caffeinated beverages, or foods containing caffeine, did you consume today? ....

At what time? ....

Medications or supplements taken today ....

.... At what time? ....

Did you exercise today? .... When, what, and for how long? ....

....

Did you take any naps? .... When, and for how long? ....

Did you eat heavy meals or spicy foods? What kinds of foods? ....

Any alcoholic beverages consumed today? .... At what time? ....

Describe your day. Was it stimulating or stressful? ....

....

How was your mood? ....

Notes ....

🌙 BEDTIME

What did you eat or drink within the last three hours? ....

What medications are you taking before bedtime? ....
Before getting ready for bed, I

☐ Took a hot bath   ☐ Read a physical printed book

☐ Meditated   ☐ Other ....

☐ Used my cell phone or other electronic device

....

Notes ....

....

....

DATE _____ DAY OF THE WEEK _____

☀ MORNING

When I went to bed last night .... When I woke up this morning ....

About how long I think it took me to fall asleep last night ....

Sleep disruptions ....

....

....

How long it took me to go back to sleep ....

Total hours I slept last night (approximate) ....

How I feel this morning

☐ Great ☐ Good ☐ Tired but functioning

☐ Very tired ☐ Not well

Notes ....

....

....

🌙 DREAMS

Describe or draw your dreams here

....

....

....

....

....

....

....

....

....

DAYTIME

How many caffeinated beverages, or foods containing caffeine, did you consume today? ....

At what time? ....

Medications or supplements taken today ....

....At what time? ....

Did you exercise today? ....When, what, and for how long? ....

....

Did you take any naps? ....When, and for how long? ....

Did you eat heavy meals or spicy foods? What kinds of foods? ....

Any alcoholic beverages consumed today? ....At what time? ....

Describe your day. Was it stimulating or stressful? ....

....

How was your mood? ....

Notes ....

BEDTIME

What did you eat or drink within the last three hours? ....

What medications are you taking before bedtime? ....

Before getting ready for bed, I

☐ Took a hot bath   ☐ Read a physical printed book

☐ Meditated   ☐ Other ....

☐ Used my cell phone or other electronic device

....

Notes ....

....

....

....

DATE _____ DAY OF THE WEEK _____

☀ MORNING

When I went to bed last night .... When I woke up this morning ....

About how long I think it took me to fall asleep last night ....

Sleep disruptions ....

....

....

How long it took me to go back to sleep ....

Total hours I slept last night (approximate) ....

How I feel this morning

☐ Great ☐ Good ☐ Tired but functioning

☐ Very tired ☐ Not well

Notes ....

....

....

🌙 DREAMS

Describe or draw your dreams here

....

....

....

....

....

....

....

....

....

....

....

....

DAYTIME

How many caffeinated beverages, or foods containing caffeine, did you consume today? ....

At what time? ....

Medications or supplements taken today ....

.... At what time? ....

Did you exercise today? .... When, what, and for how long? ....

....

Did you take any naps? .... When, and for how long? ....

Did you eat heavy meals or spicy foods? What kinds of foods? ....

Any alcoholic beverages consumed today? .... At what time? ....

Describe your day. Was it stimulating or stressful? ....

....

How was your mood? ....

Notes ....

BEDTIME

What did you eat or drink within the last three hours? ....

What medications are you taking before bedtime? ....

Before getting ready for bed, I

☐ Took a hot bath

☐ Meditated

☐ Used my cell phone or other electronic device

☐ Read a physical printed book

☐ Other ....

....

Notes ....

....

....

DATE _____ DAY OF THE WEEK _____

☀ MORNING

When I went to bed last night .... When I woke up this morning ....

About how long I think it took me to fall asleep last night ....

Sleep disruptions ....

....

....

How long it took me to go back to sleep ....

Total hours I slept last night (approximate) ....

How I feel this morning

☐ Great ☐ Good ☐ Tired but functioning

☐ Very tired ☐ Not well

Notes ....

....

....

🌙 DREAMS

Describe or draw your dreams here

....

....

....

....

....

....

....

....

....

....

 DAYTIME

How many caffeinated beverages, or foods containing caffeine, did you consume today? ....

At what time? ....

Medications or supplements taken today ....

....At what time? ....

Did you exercise today? ....When, what, and for how long? ....

....

Did you take any naps? ....When, and for how long? ....

Did you eat heavy meals or spicy foods? What kinds of foods? ....

Any alcoholic beverages consumed today? ....At what time? ....

Describe your day. Was it stimulating or stressful? ....

....

How was your mood? ....

Notes ....

BEDTIME

What did you eat or drink within the last three hours? ....

What medications are you taking before bedtime? ....

Before getting ready for bed, I

☐ Took a hot bath

☐ Meditated

☐ Used my cell phone or other electronic device

☐ Read a physical printed book

☐ Other ....

....

....

Notes ....

....

....

....

DATE _____ DAY OF THE WEEK _____

☀ MORNING

When I went to bed last night .... When I woke up this morning ....

About how long I think it took me to fall asleep last night ....

Sleep disruptions ....

....

....

How long it took me to go back to sleep ....

Total hours I slept last night (approximate) ....

How I feel this morning

☐ Great ☐ Good ☐ Tired but functioning

☐ Very tired ☐ Not well

Notes ....

....

....

🌙 DREAMS

Describe or draw your dreams here

....

....

....

....

....

....

....

....

....

DAYTIME

How many caffeinated beverages, or foods containing caffeine, did you consume today? ....

At what time? ....

Medications or supplements taken today ....

....At what time? ....

Did you exercise today? ....When, what, and for how long? ....

....

Did you take any naps? ....When, and for how long? ....

Did you eat heavy meals or spicy foods? What kinds of foods? ....

Any alcoholic beverages consumed today? .... At what time? ....

Describe your day. Was it stimulating or stressful? ....

....

How was your mood? ....

Notes ....

BEDTIME

What did you eat or drink within the last three hours? ....

What medications are you taking before bedtime? ....

Before getting ready for bed, I

☐ Took a hot bath   ☐ Read a physical printed book

☐ Meditated   ☐ Other ....

☐ Used my cell phone or other electronic device

....

....

Notes ....

....

....

....

DATE _____ DAY OF THE WEEK _____

☀ MORNING

When I went to bed last night .... When I woke up this morning ....

About how long I think it took me to fall asleep last night ....

Sleep disruptions ....

....

....

How long it took me to go back to sleep ....

Total hours I slept last night (approximate) ....

How I feel this morning

☐ Great   ☐ Good   ☐ Tired but functioning

☐ Very tired   ☐ Not well

Notes ....

....

....

☾ DREAMS

Describe or draw your dreams here

....

....

....

....

....

....

....

....

 # DAYTIME

How many caffeinated beverages, or foods containing caffeine, did you consume today? ....

At what time? ....

Medications or supplements taken today ....

....................At what time? ....

Did you exercise today? ....When, what, and for how long? ....

....

Did you take any naps? ....When, and for how long? ....

Did you eat heavy meals or spicy foods? What kinds of foods? ....

Any alcoholic beverages consumed today? ....At what time? ....

Describe your day. Was it stimulating or stressful? ....

....

How was your mood? ....

Notes ....

BEDTIME

What did you eat or drink within the last three hours? ....

What medications are you taking before bedtime? ....

Before getting ready for bed, I

☐ Took a hot bath

☐ Meditated

☐ Used my cell phone or other electronic device

☐ Read a physical printed book

☐ Other ....

....

....

Notes ....

....

....

....

DATE _____ DAY OF THE WEEK _____

☀ MORNING

When I went to bed last night .... When I woke up this morning ....

About how long I think it took me to fall asleep last night ....

Sleep disruptions ....

....

....

How long it took me to go back to sleep ....

Total hours I slept last night (approximate) ....

How I feel this morning

☐ Great   ☐ Good   ☐ Tired but functioning

☐ Very tired   ☐ Not well

Notes ....

....

....

🌙 DREAMS

Describe or draw your dreams here

....

....

....

....

....

....

....

....

....

 # DAYTIME

How many caffeinated beverages, or foods containing caffeine, did you consume today? ....

At what time? ....

Medications or supplements taken today ....

....At what time? ....

Did you exercise today? ....When, what, and for how long? ....

....

Did you take any naps? ....When, and for how long? ....

Did you eat heavy meals or spicy foods? What kinds of foods? ....

Any alcoholic beverages consumed today? ....At what time? ....

Describe your day. Was it stimulating or stressful? ....

....

How was your mood? ....

Notes ....

BEDTIME

What did you eat or drink within the last three hours? ....

What medications are you taking before bedtime? ....
Before getting ready for bed, I

☐ Took a hot bath

☐ Meditated

☐ Used my cell phone or other electronic device

☐ Read a physical printed book

☐ Other ....

....

....

Notes ....

....

....

DATE _____ DAY OF THE WEEK _____

☀ MORNING

When I went to bed last night .... When I woke up this morning ....

About how long I think it took me to fall asleep last night ....

Sleep disruptions ....

....

....

How long it took me to go back to sleep ....

Total hours I slept last night (approximate) ....

How I feel this morning

☐ Great   ☐ Good   ☐ Tired but functioning

☐ Very tired   ☐ Not well

Notes ....

....

....

☁ DREAMS

Describe or draw your dreams here

....

....

....

....

....

....

....

....

....

....

DAYTIME

How many caffeinated beverages, or foods containing caffeine, did you consume today? ....

At what time? ....

Medications or supplements taken today ....

.... At what time? ....

Did you exercise today? .... When, what, and for how long? ....

....

Did you take any naps? .... When, and for how long? ....

Did you eat heavy meals or spicy foods? What kinds of foods? ....

Any alcoholic beverages consumed today? .... At what time? ....

Describe your day. Was it stimulating or stressful? ....

....

How was your mood? ....

Notes ....

BEDTIME

What did you eat or drink within the last three hours? ....

What medications are you taking before bedtime? ....

Before getting ready for bed, I

☐ Took a hot bath

☐ Meditated

☐ Used my cell phone or other electronic device

☐ Read a physical printed book

☐ Other ....

....

Notes ....

....

....

....

DATE _____ DAY OF THE WEEK _____

☀ MORNING

When I went to bed last night .... When I woke up this morning ....

About how long I think it took me to fall asleep last night ....

Sleep disruptions ....

....

....

How long it took me to go back to sleep ....

Total hours I slept last night (approximate) ....

How I feel this morning

☐ Great   ☐ Good   ☐ Tired but functioning

☐ Very tired   ☐ Not well

Notes ....

....

....

☾ DREAMS

Describe or draw your dreams here

....

....

....

....

....

....

....

....

....

DAYTIME

How many caffeinated beverages, or foods containing caffeine, did you consume today? ....

At what time? ....

Medications or supplements taken today ....

....At what time? ....

Did you exercise today? ....When, what, and for how long? ....

....

Did you take any naps? .... When, and for how long? ....

Did you eat heavy meals or spicy foods? What kinds of foods? ....

Any alcoholic beverages consumed today? ....At what time? ....

Describe your day. Was it stimulating or stressful? ....

....

How was your mood? ....

Notes ....

BEDTIME

What did you eat or drink within the last three hours? ....

What medications are you taking before bedtime? ....

Before getting ready for bed, I

☐ Took a hot bath

☐ Meditated

☐ Used my cell phone or other electronic device

☐ Read a physical printed book

☐ Other ....

....

....

Notes ....

....

....

....

DATE _____ DAY OF THE WEEK _____

☀ MORNING

When I went to bed last night ....When I woke up this morning ....

About how long I think it took me to fall asleep last night ....

Sleep disruptions ....

....

....

How long it took me to go back to sleep ....

Total hours I slept last night (approximate) ....

How I feel this morning

☐ Great   ☐ Good   ☐ Tired but functioning

☐ Very tired   ☐ Not well

Notes ....

....

....

☾ DREAMS

Describe or draw your dreams here

....

....

....

....

....

....

....

....

....

# DAYTIME

How many caffeinated beverages, or foods containing caffeine, did you consume today? ....

At what time? ....

Medications or supplements taken today ....

....At what time? ....

Did you exercise today? .... When, what, and for how long? ....

....

Did you take any naps? .... When, and for how long? ....

Did you eat heavy meals or spicy foods? What kinds of foods? ....

Any alcoholic beverages consumed today? .... At what time? ....

Describe your day. Was it stimulating or stressful? ....

....

How was your mood? ....

Notes ....

BEDTIME

What did you eat or drink within the last three hours? ....

What medications are you taking before bedtime? ....

Before getting ready for bed, I

☐ Took a hot bath   ☐ Read a physical printed book

☐ Meditated   ☐ Other ....

☐ Used my cell phone or other electronic device   ....

....

Notes ....

....

....

DATE _____ DAY OF THE WEEK _____

☀ MORNING

When I went to bed last night .... When I woke up this morning ....

About how long I think it took me to fall asleep last night ....

Sleep disruptions ....

....

....

How long it took me to go back to sleep ....

Total hours I slept last night (approximate) ....

How I feel this morning

☐ Great　　☐ Good　　☐ Tired but functioning

☐ Very tired　　☐ Not well

Notes ....

....

....

☾ DREAMS

Describe or draw your dreams here

....

....

....

....

....

....

....

....

# DAYTIME

How many caffeinated beverages, or foods containing caffeine, did you consume today? ....

At what time? ....

Medications or supplements taken today ....

....At what time? ....

Did you exercise today? .... When, what, and for how long? ....

....

Did you take any naps? .... When, and for how long? ....

Did you eat heavy meals or spicy foods? What kinds of foods? ....

Any alcoholic beverages consumed today? .... At what time? ....

Describe your day. Was it stimulating or stressful? ....

....

How was your mood? ....

Notes ....

BEDTIME

What did you eat or drink within the last three hours? ....

What medications are you taking before bedtime? ....
Before getting ready for bed, I

☐ Took a hot bath   ☐ Read a physical printed book

☐ Meditated   ☐ Other ....

☐ Used my cell phone or other electronic device

....

Notes ....

....

....

ADJUSTMENTS TO MAKE/THINGS TO TRY

ADJUSTMENTS TO MAKE/THINGS TO TRY

ADJUSTMENTS TO MAKE/THINGS TO TRY

RESOURCES

FOR MORE INFORMATION TO HELP YOU REST EASY, CHECK OUT THESE RESOURCES:

National Sleep Foundation: https://sleepfoundation.org
The U.S. National Sleep Foundation is dedicated to improving health and well-being through sleep education and advocacy.

The Sleep Council: www.sleepcouncil.org.uk
The U.K. Sleep Council offers advice and guidance on healthy sleep habits.

U.S. Department of Health and Human Services, National Institutes of Health, National Heart, Lung, and Blood Institute: http://www.nhlbi.nih.gov/

Llewellyn's Complete Dictionary of Dreams by Dr. Michael Lennox. Woodbury, Minnesota: Llewellyn Publications, 2015.

The Sleep Revolution: Transforming Your Life, One Night at a Time by Arianna Huffington. New York: Harmony Books, 2016.

Sleep Soundly Every Night, Feel Fantastic Every Day: A Doctor's Guide to Solving Your Sleep Problems by Robert S. Rosenberg, DO, FCCP. New York: Demos Health, 2014.

Sleep Smarter: 21 Essential Strategies to Sleep Your Way to a Better Body, Better Health, and Bigger Success by Shawn Stevenson. New York: Rodale Wellness, 2016.